MW01001706

50 Uses for Your Dog

Written by

Jay Groce
Francesca Peppiatt
Paul Seaburn

new seasons®

1   To help you search for that missing sock

2 🐾 To keep a secret, no matter how dog-gone juicy

3 🐾 To remind you that you can't buy "cute" at a toy store

4

To make sure you don't bark up the wrong tree

5 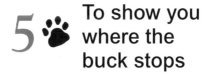 To show you where the buck stops

6

 To hide stains on the furniture when company comes over

7 🐾 To dig what you've done with the garden

8 🐾 To remind you what Saturdays are for

9 🐾 To pull for you when the blues threaten to attack

10 🐾 To listen when you feel like screaming

11  To remind you that friends come in many different shapes and sizes

12 🐾 To lick that junk mail problem . . .

. . . once and for all

13 To give you a
new "leash"
on life

14

To demonstrate that some things are good to the last drop

15 🐾 To make sure no one sees the strained-pea handoff

16 To keep the cat on its toes

17 🐾 To cheer up a benchwarmer

18 🐾 To help you through rocky times

19 🐾 To share a lazy summer afternoon

21 🐾 To prove everyone is ticklish somewhere

22  To manage your 401-K9

23 🐾 To help out when the dishwasher breaks

To make you feel better about those laugh lines

25 🐾 To put the "pup" in pup tent

26 🐾 To watch the cat's every move

28 🐾 To give new meaning to the phrase "just chillin'"

29 🐾 To keep the carrier warm while the baby is being changed

30 🐾 To make sure you get out—even when it's snowing

31  To pitch in when the whirlpool is broken

32 🐾 To form an alliance to vote the ferret out of the tribe

33 🐾 To be an anchor on windy days

34 To stick up for an ugly duckling

35 🐾 To be by your side—whether the seas are calm or stormy

36 🐾 To give you an
excuse for not
jogging today

37 🐾 To screen your calls

38 🐾 To support (if not approve of) your decision to get a cat

39 🐾 To give you a
heads-up
when it's time
for a diaper
change

40  To be on the lookout for the nearest fire hydrant

41 🐾 To cheer up the crabgrass

42 🐾 To take the blame when you don't feel like making the bed

43 🐾 **To illustrate the term *dog tired***

44  To fill in for the Easter Bunny

45 🐾 To guard the chimney from imposters

To stay and clean up after the party

47 🐾 To keep an eye on the neighbors

48 🐾 To test your raft for leaks

49 🐾 To prove that the grass is greener on your side of the fence

50 🐾 To take the edge off a hard day